Chapter 1: Understanding Democracy

What is Democracy?

Democracy is a concept that is often talked about in the realm of politics, but what exactly does it mean? At its core, democracy is a form of government in which power is vested in the people, who rule either directly or through elected representatives. It is a system that values individual rights, freedom of speech, and the ability for citizens to participate in decision-making processes.

In a democratic society, the government is accountable to the people through elections and other mechanisms of oversight. This means that leaders are chosen by the people and can be replaced if they do not uphold the values and interests of the population. Democracy also promotes the idea of equality, as all individuals are considered equal under the law and have the right to participate in the political process.

One key aspect of democracy is the protection of minority rights. In a true democracy, the rights of minorities are respected and upheld, even if they are not in the majority. This ensures that all individuals are able to express their opinions and have a voice in shaping the direction of the country. It is this commitment to inclusivity and diversity that sets democracy apart from other forms of government.

In the United States, democracy is enshrined in the Constitution and is the foundation of the country's political system. Through a system of checks and balances, the government is designed to prevent any one branch from becoming too powerful and to ensure that the rights of individuals are protected. The principles of democracy are reflected in the Bill of Rights, which guarantees freedoms such as speech, religion, and assembly.

Overall, democracy is a system of government that values the input and participation of its citizens. It is a way to ensure that the government works for the people and not the other way around. By understanding the principles of democracy and actively engaging in the political process, individuals can help shape the future of their country and ensure that their voices are heard.

The History of Democracy in America

The history of democracy in America is a fascinating journey that spans centuries and has shaped the very foundation of our nation. From the early colonial days to the present day, the principles of democracy have played a pivotal role in shaping our government and society.

The roots of democracy in America can be traced back to the early colonial period, when settlers sought to establish self-governing communities based on principles of equality and representation. The Mayflower Compact of 1620, for example, laid the groundwork for democratic governance by establishing a framework for self-rule among the Pilgrims who settled in Plymouth, Massachusetts.

As America grew and evolved, so too did its commitment to democratic principles. The Declaration of Independence, penned by Thomas Jefferson in 1776, boldly proclaimed that all men are created equal and endowed with certain unalienable rights, including life, liberty, and the pursuit of happiness. This declaration of individual rights and freedoms laid the groundwork for the democratic ideals that would come to define American society.

The establishment of the United States Constitution in 1787 further solidified America's commitment to democracy by creating a system of government based on the principles of separation of powers, checks and balances, and the protection of individual rights. The Constitution has served as the bedrock of American democracy for over two centuries, providing a framework for governance that has withstood the test of time.

Today, the legacy of democracy in America continues to shape our government, society, and culture. As we navigate the complexities of modern politics and society, it is important to remember the rich history of democracy in America and the enduring principles that have guided our nation since its inception. By understanding the history of democracy in America, we can better appreciate the importance of civic engagement, political participation, and the preservation of our democratic institutions for future generations.

The Principles of Democracy

Democracy is a system of government that is founded on certain key principles. In this subchapter, we will explore the fundamental principles of democracy that are at the core of American politics. Understanding these principles is essential for every citizen, as they form the foundation of our political system and guide how our government operates.

The first principle of democracy is the idea of popular sovereignty, which means that the power of the government comes from the people. In a democracy, the people are the ultimate authority, and they have the right to choose their leaders through free and fair elections. This principle ensures that elected officials are accountable to the people and must govern in accordance with their wishes.

Another important principle of democracy is the rule of law, which means that all individuals and institutions are subject to the law. This principle ensures that everyone is treated equally under the law and that no one is above it. The rule of law protects individual rights and ensures that government actions are limited by the law.

Transparency and accountability are also key principles of democracy. Citizens have the right to access information about government actions and decisions, and elected officials are accountable to the people for their actions. Transparency and accountability help to prevent corruption and ensure that government operates in the best interests of the people.

In a democracy, the protection of individual rights is paramount. The Constitution guarantees certain rights and freedoms to all citizens, such as freedom of speech, religion, and assembly. These rights are essential to democracy, as they ensure that individuals can express themselves freely and participate in the political process without fear of retribution.

Finally, democracy is built on the principle of compromise and consensus-building. In a diverse society like the United States, it is important for different groups and interests to come together to make decisions that benefit the greater good. Compromise and consensus-building are essential for a functioning democracy, as they ensure that all voices are heard and considered in the decision-making process. By upholding these principles of democracy, we can ensure that our government remains of the people, by the people, and for the people.

Chapter 2: The American Political System

The Three Branches of Government

In the United States, the government is divided into three separate branches: the executive branch, the legislative branch, and the judicial branch. Each branch has its own unique responsibilities and powers, which are outlined in the United States Constitution. Understanding the roles and functions of these branches is essential for anyone who wants to understand how our government operates.

The executive branch is headed by the President of the United States and includes the Vice President, the Cabinet, and various federal agencies. The President is responsible for enforcing the laws passed by Congress, as well as making important decisions regarding foreign policy, the military, and the economy. The executive branch also has the power to veto legislation passed by Congress, although Congress can override a veto with a two-thirds majority vote.

The legislative branch, also known as Congress, is responsible for making the laws of the land. Congress is divided into two chambers:

the House of Representatives and the Senate. Members of Congress are elected by the people and are responsible for representing the interests of their constituents. Congress has the power to declare war, raise taxes, and regulate commerce, among other important functions.

The judicial branch is made up of the federal courts, including the Supreme Court. The judiciary is responsible for interpreting the laws and ensuring that they are applied fairly and consistently. The Supreme Court has the power to review laws passed by Congress and actions taken by the President to determine their constitutionality. This power, known as judicial review, is a crucial check on the other branches of government.

Overall, the three branches of government work together to ensure that the United States remains a functioning democracy. By dividing power among these branches and providing a system of checks and balances, the framers of the Constitution sought to prevent any one branch from becoming too powerful. Understanding the roles and responsibilities of each branch is essential for anyone who wants to fully participate in our democratic system.

The Role of the President

In the United States, the President plays a crucial role in shaping the direction of the country and representing the interests of its citizens. The President serves as the head of state and government, responsible for implementing and enforcing the laws of the land. This position holds significant power and influence, as the President is the commander-in-chief of the armed forces and has the authority to make important decisions on domestic and foreign policy matters.

One of the primary responsibilities of the President is to serve as the chief executive of the federal government. This means that the President is responsible for overseeing the various executive branch agencies and departments, ensuring that they are carrying out the laws and policies of the country. The President also has the power to appoint key officials, such as cabinet members and federal judges, who help to shape the direction of the government and its policies.

Another important role of the President is to serve as the chief diplomat of the United States. The President has the authority to negotiate treaties with foreign countries, appoint ambassadors, and represent the United States on the world stage. This role is crucial in maintaining strong relationships with other countries and promoting the interests of the United States in the global community.

The President also plays a key role in the legislative process, as outlined in the Constitution. While Congress is responsible for passing laws, the President has the power to veto legislation, which can prevent a bill from becoming law. The President can also propose legislation to Congress and use the bully pulpit to influence public opinion and build support for their policy agenda.

Overall, the role of the President is multifaceted and complex, requiring a deep understanding of the political process and the ability to navigate the challenges of governing a diverse and complex country. The President must balance the needs and interests of the American people while also representing the United States on the world stage. By fulfilling these responsibilities effectively, the

President can help to shape the future of the country and ensure that the principles of democracy are upheld.

The Role of Congress

The Role of Congress is vital in the functioning of American democracy. As the legislative branch of the government, Congress is responsible for making laws, overseeing the budget, and representing the people of the United States. Comprised of two chambers, the House of Representatives and the Senate, Congress plays a crucial role in the checks and balances system, ensuring that no one branch of government becomes too powerful.

One of the primary functions of Congress is to create laws that govern the country. This process begins with a bill, which can be introduced by any member of Congress. The bill then goes through a series of steps, including committee hearings and debates, before being voted on by both chambers. If the bill passes both the House and the Senate, it is sent to the President for approval. This process ensures that laws are carefully considered and debated before being enacted.

In addition to creating laws, Congress is also responsible for overseeing the federal budget. Each year, Congress must pass a budget that outlines how federal funds will be allocated. This process involves extensive negotiations and debates, as members of Congress work to balance competing priorities and ensure that taxpayer dollars are spent responsibly. Through the budget process, Congress has the power to influence government spending and shape national priorities.

Another important role of Congress is to represent the interests of the American people. Members of Congress are elected to represent specific districts or states, and it is their responsibility to listen to their constituents and advocate for their needs and concerns. Through constituent services and town hall meetings, members of Congress work to stay connected to the people they represent and ensure that their voices are heard in the halls of power.

Overall, the role of Congress is essential in American democracy. By creating laws, overseeing the budget, and representing the people, Congress plays a crucial role in shaping the direction of the country. As citizens, it is important to understand the role of Congress and hold our elected officials accountable for their actions. By staying informed and engaged in the political process, we can help ensure that Congress fulfills its duty to the American people.

The Role of the Supreme Court

The Supreme Court plays a crucial role in shaping American democracy by interpreting the Constitution and ensuring that laws align with its principles. As the highest court in the land, the Supreme Court has the power to review laws passed by Congress and actions taken by the executive branch to determine their constitutionality. This process, known as judicial review, allows the Court to uphold or strike down laws that are found to be in violation of the Constitution.

One of the key functions of the Supreme Court is to protect individual rights and liberties guaranteed by the Constitution. Through landmark decisions such as Brown v. Board of Education, Roe v. Wade, and Obergefell v. Hodges, the Court has played a pivotal role in advancing civil rights, reproductive rights, and marriage equality in the United States. By interpreting the Constitution in a way that reflects the changing values and norms of society, the Court helps to ensure that all Americans have equal protection under the law.

In addition to safeguarding individual rights, the Supreme Court also serves as a check on the power of the other branches of government. Through its ability to strike down unconstitutional laws and executive actions, the Court helps to maintain the system of checks and balances that is essential to American democracy. By holding the government accountable to the principles laid out in the Constitution, the Court helps to prevent the concentration of power in any one branch.

The Supreme Court is composed of nine justices who are appointed

for life by the President with the advice and consent of the Senate.

This lifetime appointment ensures that the Court remains

independent and free from political influence, allowing the justices

to make decisions based on the law rather than partisan interests.

While the Court is not immune to political considerations, its

commitment to upholding the Constitution as the supreme law of the

land helps to maintain its credibility and legitimacy in the eyes of the

American people.

Overall, the Supreme Court plays a critical role in American politics

by interpreting the Constitution, protecting individual rights, and

serving as a check on the power of the other branches of

government. By upholding the principles of democracy and the rule

of law, the Court helps to ensure that the rights and liberties of all

Americans are protected and that the government operates within the

bounds of the Constitution. As citizens, it is important to understand

the role of the Supreme Court and the impact it has on our daily lives

as we navigate the complexities of American politics.

Chapter 3: Elections and Political Parties

How Elections Work in America

In America, elections play a crucial role in shaping the country's political landscape. Understanding how elections work is essential for all citizens to actively participate in the democratic process. In this subchapter, we will break down the fundamentals of how elections work in America, providing a simple guide for the average person, teachers, and students.

First and foremost, the election process begins with the selection of candidates. Political parties hold primary elections or caucuses to choose their nominees for various offices, including the presidency, Congress, and state and local positions. During these primary elections, registered party members vote for their preferred candidate, who will represent the party in the general election.

Once the candidates are selected, the general election takes place. In this phase, all registered voters are eligible to cast their ballots for their preferred candidate. The candidate who receives the majority of votes in the general election wins the office. In some cases, if no candidate receives a majority, a runoff election may be held to determine the winner.

It's important to note that the American electoral system operates on a winner-takes-all basis in most elections. This means that the candidate who receives the most votes wins the election, regardless of the margin of victory. However, in some cases, such as presidential elections, the Electoral College comes into play, where each state has a certain number of electoral votes based on its population.

In conclusion, understanding how elections work in America is essential for all citizens to actively participate in the democratic process. By familiarizing yourself with the election process, you can make informed decisions when casting your vote and contribute to shaping the future of the country. Whether you are an average person, teacher, or student, this simple guide to American politics will help you navigate the complexities of the electoral system with ease.

The Two-Party System

In the United States, the two-party system has long been a defining feature of American politics. The two major parties, the Democrats and the Republicans, dominate the political landscape and play a crucial role in shaping the country's policies and governing institutions. Understanding the two-party system is essential for anyone looking to navigate the complexities of American politics.

The two-party system in the United States can be traced back to the early days of the republic. The Federalists and the Democratic-Republicans were the first two major parties, and their rivalry laid the foundation for the modern two-party system. Over time, these parties evolved into the Democrats and the Republicans, who have been the dominant political forces in the country for the past century.

One of the key features of the two-party system is its tendency to promote a binary view of politics. Voters are often presented with a choice between the two major parties, which can lead to a lack of diversity in political opinions and ideas. This can be frustrating for voters who feel that neither party represents their views, but the two-party system has proven to be remarkably resilient over the years.

Despite its drawbacks, the two-party system has several advantages. For one, it helps to promote stability and continuity in government. With two major parties competing for power, there is a built-in system of checks and balances that prevents any one party from becoming too dominant. Additionally, the two-party system encourages compromise and cooperation between different political factions, which can lead to more effective governance.

In conclusion, the two-party system is a fundamental aspect of American politics that shapes the way our government functions. While it has its limitations, the two-party system has endured for centuries and continues to play a central role in the political life of the nation. Understanding how the two-party system operates is essential for anyone looking to engage with the complexities of American politics and make informed decisions as a citizen.

Third Parties in American Politics

Third parties in American politics play a crucial role in shaping the political landscape, despite often being overshadowed by the two major parties, the Democrats and Republicans. These third parties provide alternative perspectives and ideas that may not be represented by the mainstream parties, giving voters more choices and diversifying the political discourse. While third parties rarely win national elections, they can still influence the political agenda and push for important policy changes.

One of the most well-known third parties in American history is the Libertarian Party, which advocates for limited government intervention in both economic and social issues. The Green Party, on the other hand, focuses on environmental sustainability and social justice. These third parties attract voters who may not feel represented by the policies of the major parties, and serve as a voice for marginalized communities and alternative viewpoints.

Despite their important role in American politics, third parties face significant obstacles in gaining traction and winning elections. The two-party system in the United States makes it difficult for third parties to compete on a level playing field, as the major parties have established networks of support and resources that are difficult for third parties to match. Additionally, many voters feel pressured to vote for one of the major party candidates in order to prevent the candidate they dislike from winning, leading to a cycle of limited support for third parties.

However, third parties can still have a significant impact on American politics even without winning elections. By bringing attention to important issues and pushing for policy changes, third parties can influence the platforms of the major parties and shape the national conversation. In some cases, third party candidates have even been able to swing elections by siphoning off votes from one of the major party candidates, highlighting the potential power of third parties in American politics.

In conclusion, third parties play a crucial role in American politics by providing alternative perspectives and ideas that may not be represented by the major parties. While they face significant obstacles in gaining traction and winning elections, third parties can

still influence the political agenda and push for important policy

changes. By supporting third parties and giving them a platform to

voice their ideas, voters can help diversify the political discourse and

ensure that all voices are heard in the democratic process.

Chapter 4: The Role of the Media

The Influence of the Media on Politics

The media plays a crucial role in shaping the political landscape in America. From news coverage to social media platforms, the influence of the media on politics cannot be overstated. In this subchapter, we will explore how the media impacts political discourse and decision-making in the United States.

One of the most significant ways in which the media influences politics is through its coverage of political events and issues. News outlets play a vital role in informing the public about current events, government policies, and political debates. The way in which the media frames these stories can shape public opinion and influence political outcomes. For example, biased reporting or sensationalist headlines can sway public perception of a particular candidate or policy.

Social media has also emerged as a powerful tool for political communication and influence. Platforms like Twitter, Facebook, and

Instagram allow politicians to reach a wide audience instantly and engage with voters in real-time. However, the spread of misinformation and fake news on social media has raised concerns about the impact of these platforms on political discourse. It is essential for consumers of media to critically evaluate the information they receive and verify the sources before forming opinions on political issues.

In addition to shaping public opinion, the media also plays a role in holding politicians and government officials accountable. Investigative journalism uncovers corruption, misconduct, and abuse of power within the government, leading to greater transparency and accountability. Without a free and independent press, democracy cannot thrive, as citizens rely on the media to keep them informed about the actions of their elected representatives.

Overall, the influence of the media on politics is undeniable. It is essential for the average person, teachers, and students to be aware of how the media shapes political discourse and decision-making in America. By staying informed, critically evaluating information, and holding media outlets accountable for their reporting, we can ensure that the media serves as a watchdog for democracy and promotes an informed and engaged citizenry.

How to Identify Bias in the Media

In today's digital age, it is more important than ever to be able to identify bias in the media. Bias refers to a preference or inclination towards a particular perspective, ideology, or group. This bias can impact the way information is presented and can influence our understanding of current events and issues. By being able to recognize bias in the media, we can better navigate the vast amount of information available to us and make more informed decisions.

One way to identify bias in the media is to pay attention to the language used in news articles or broadcasts. Look for loaded or emotional language that is designed to evoke a specific reaction from the audience. Words like "shocking," "outrageous," or "scandalous" may indicate a bias towards a particular viewpoint. Additionally, watch out for generalizations or stereotypes that oversimplify complex issues.

Another way to spot bias in the media is to consider the sources of information being cited. Are the sources reputable and trustworthy, or are they known for promoting a particular agenda? It is important to fact-check information and be wary of sources that have a history of spreading misinformation. Additionally, consider the diversity of perspectives presented in the media. Are all sides of an issue being represented, or is the coverage one-sided?

It is also important to be aware of the context in which information is presented. Pay attention to the framing of stories and the selection of images or video footage. Is the information being presented in a fair and balanced manner, or is it being manipulated to convey a particular message? By being mindful of how information is being presented, we can better evaluate its credibility and potential bias.

Lastly, it is crucial to be aware of the financial interests behind media outlets. Consider who owns the media organization and what their motivations may be. Are they driven by profit, political ideology, or other factors that may influence the content they produce? By understanding the financial incentives at play, we can better assess the potential bias of a media source.

By being vigilant and critical consumers of media, we can better protect ourselves from the influence of bias and misinformation. By following these tips and strategies, we can navigate the complex landscape of media and make more informed decisions about the information we consume.

The Importance of Media Literacy

In today's digital age, the importance of media literacy cannot be overstated. With the proliferation of news sources and the rise of social media, it has become increasingly challenging to discern fact from fiction. Media literacy is the ability to critically analyze and evaluate the information we consume, whether it be from traditional news outlets or social media platforms. In order to be informed citizens and active participants in a democracy, it is crucial that we develop strong media literacy skills.

Media literacy is essential for the average person to navigate the vast amount of information available to us on a daily basis. With the rise of fake news and misinformation, being able to discern credible sources from unreliable ones is more important than ever. By developing media literacy skills, individuals can protect themselves from falling prey to false information and make more informed decisions about the world around them.

For teachers, media literacy is a crucial tool for educating students about the complexities of the media landscape. By teaching students how to critically evaluate sources and analyze media messages, educators can empower the next generation to be discerning consumers of information. Media literacy education can help students develop the skills they need to be active participants in a democracy and engage critically with the media they encounter.

Students, in particular, stand to benefit greatly from developing strong media literacy skills. In a world where information is constantly bombarding us from all angles, being able to sift through the noise and identify reliable sources is a valuable skill. By teaching students how to critically analyze media messages and question the information they encounter, educators can help them become more informed and engaged citizens.

In conclusion, media literacy is a vital skill that is necessary for navigating the complexities of the modern media landscape. By developing strong media literacy skills, individuals can protect themselves from misinformation, make more informed decisions, and actively participate in a democratic society. For the average person, teachers, and students alike, media literacy is an essential tool for understanding and engaging with the world around us.

Chapter 5: Civic Engagement

Why Civic Engagement is Important

Civic engagement is crucial for maintaining a healthy democracy. It allows citizens to participate in the political process, make their voices heard, and hold their elected officials accountable. By engaging in activities such as voting, contacting elected representatives, and participating in community events, individuals can help shape the policies and decisions that impact their lives. In this subchapter, we will explore why civic engagement is important and how it can benefit both individuals and society as a whole.

One of the main reasons why civic engagement is important is that it helps to ensure that the government is responsive to the needs and concerns of the people. When citizens actively participate in the political process, they can influence the decisions that are made by their elected officials. This can help to create a more responsive and accountable government that truly represents the will of the people. By staying informed, getting involved, and speaking up, individuals can help to shape the policies and priorities of their community, state, and nation.

Another reason why civic engagement is important is that it helps to build a sense of community and connection among individuals. When people come together to work towards a common goal, whether it be through volunteering, attending a town hall meeting, or participating in a protest, they can form bonds with others who share their values and beliefs. This sense of community can help to foster a greater sense of belonging and unity, which is essential for a healthy and vibrant society.

Civic engagement also plays a crucial role in promoting social justice and equality. When individuals speak out against injustice, advocate for marginalized communities, and work to address systemic issues, they can help to create a more just and equitable society for all. By raising awareness, mobilizing support, and pushing for change, civic engagement can help to address issues such as poverty, discrimination, and inequality, and promote a more inclusive and fair society for everyone.

In conclusion, civic engagement is essential for a healthy democracy and a thriving society. By actively participating in the political process, individuals can help to shape the policies and decisions that impact their lives, build a sense of community and connection with others, and promote social justice and equality. Whether you are an average person, a teacher, or a student, it is important to recognize the power of civic engagement and to get involved in ways that align with your values and beliefs. Democracy is not a spectator sport – it requires active participation from all of us to truly flourish.

How to Get Involved in Your Community

Getting involved in your community is an essential part of being an active and informed citizen. By participating in local events and organizations, you can make a positive impact and help shape the future of your neighborhood, town, or city. In this subchapter, we will discuss some practical ways for the average person, teachers, and students to get involved in their communities and become more engaged in the democratic process.

One way to get involved in your community is to join a local community organization or volunteer group. These groups often work on projects that benefit the community, such as cleaning up parks, organizing events, or advocating for specific issues. By joining a community organization, you can meet like-minded individuals, build relationships, and make a difference in your neighborhood.

Another way to get involved in your community is to attend local government meetings and events. By staying informed about what is happening in your town or city, you can better understand the issues facing your community and how you can contribute to positive change. Attending town hall meetings, city council meetings, and community forums is a great way to voice your opinions, ask questions, and learn more about the decision-making process.

For teachers, getting involved in the community can also be a valuable learning experience for students. By incorporating community service projects, field trips, and guest speakers into your curriculum, you can help students develop a sense of civic responsibility and an understanding of how government works. Encouraging students to get involved in their communities can also help them develop important skills such as teamwork, communication, and problem-solving.

Students can also take the initiative to get involved in their communities outside of the classroom. By volunteering at local organizations, participating in youth councils, or organizing community events, students can make a positive impact and gain valuable experience. Getting involved in the community can also help students build their resumes, develop leadership skills, and make connections with mentors and peers who share their interests.

In summary, getting involved in your community is a rewarding and important way to become more engaged in the democratic process. Whether you are an average person, teacher, or student, there are many ways to get involved and make a positive impact in your community. By joining community organizations, attending government meetings, and participating in community service projects, you can help shape the future of your neighborhood, town, or city and contribute to a more vibrant and inclusive democracy.

The Importance of Voting

Voting is a fundamental aspect of democracy and plays a crucial role in shaping the future of our country. It is not only a right but also a responsibility that every eligible citizen should take seriously. The importance of voting cannot be overstated, as it is the primary way for individuals to have a say in who represents them and the policies that will affect their lives.

One of the key reasons why voting is so important is that it gives people a voice in the decision-making process. By participating in elections, individuals can choose the candidates and policies that align with their values and beliefs. This ensures that the government represents the diverse perspectives and interests of the population, leading to more inclusive and equitable policies.

Moreover, voting is a way to hold elected officials accountable for their actions. When citizens exercise their right to vote, they send a clear message to politicians about what they expect from them. By electing representatives who prioritize the needs of the people, individuals can ensure that their voices are heard and that their concerns are addressed.

In addition, voting is a way to promote civic engagement and participation in the democratic process. When people take the time to educate themselves about the candidates and issues, they become more informed and engaged citizens. This not only strengthens our democracy but also fosters a sense of community and collective responsibility.

Overall, the importance of voting cannot be understated. It is a fundamental right and responsibility that every eligible citizen should take seriously. By participating in elections, individuals can have a say in who represents them and the policies that will affect their lives. Voting is a way to ensure that the government reflects the will of the people and promotes civic engagement and participation in the democratic process.

Chapter 6: Current Issues in American Politics

Healthcare

Healthcare is a critical issue in American politics, as it affects every individual in the country. The healthcare system in the United States is complex and often confusing, with various stakeholders and interests at play. Understanding the basics of healthcare policy is essential for citizens to make informed decisions and advocate for their own health and well-being.

One of the key concepts in American healthcare is the idea of universal coverage. Universal coverage means that every individual in the country has access to affordable healthcare services. This can take the form of government-provided healthcare, private insurance, or a combination of both. The debate over how to achieve universal coverage is a central issue in American politics, with different parties and interest groups advocating for different approaches.

Another important aspect of healthcare policy is the role of government regulation. The government plays a significant role in regulating the healthcare industry, from setting standards for healthcare providers to overseeing insurance companies. Government regulations are designed to ensure that healthcare services are safe, effective, and accessible to all individuals. However, the extent of government regulation in healthcare is a contentious issue, with some arguing for more government involvement and others advocating for less.

Cost is also a major concern in American healthcare. Healthcare costs in the United States are among the highest in the world, and many individuals struggle to afford necessary medical care. The high cost of healthcare is a barrier to access for many Americans, leading to disparities in health outcomes based on income and socioeconomic status. Addressing healthcare costs is a complex issue that requires cooperation between government, healthcare providers, and insurance companies.

Overall, healthcare is a multifaceted issue in American politics that impacts every individual in the country. Understanding the basics of healthcare policy is essential for citizens to advocate for their own health and well-being. By learning about concepts such as universal coverage, government regulation, and healthcare costs, individuals can become informed advocates for a healthcare system that meets the needs of all Americans.

Immigration

Immigration is a hot-button issue in American politics, with debates raging over border security, pathways to citizenship, and the overall impact of immigration on the country. In this subchapter, we will explore the complexities of immigration in the United States and provide a simple guide to understanding the various aspects of this contentious issue.

One of the key factors driving immigration to the United States is the pursuit of economic opportunities. Many immigrants come to the country in search of better job prospects and higher wages than they can find in their home countries. This has led to the creation of a diverse workforce in the United States, with immigrants playing a vital role in sectors such as agriculture, construction, and technology.

Another important aspect of immigration is family reunification. Many immigrants come to the United States to be reunited with family members who are already living in the country. The family-based immigration system allows U.S. citizens and lawful permanent residents to sponsor certain family members for visas, leading to the reunification of families across borders.

Immigration also plays a significant role in shaping the cultural landscape of the United States. Immigrants bring with them their own languages, traditions, and customs, enriching the country's cultural tapestry. This diversity has led to the creation of vibrant communities and has contributed to the overall strength and resilience of American society.

Despite the many benefits of immigration, the issue remains highly contentious, with debates centering around border security, the legal status of undocumented immigrants, and the overall impact of immigration on the economy and society. By understanding the complexities of immigration and the various factors driving it, we can engage in informed discussions and work towards finding solutions that are fair and just for all involved.

Climate Change

Climate change is one of the most pressing issues facing our world today. The scientific consensus is clear: the Earth's climate is changing at an unprecedented rate, largely due to human activities such as burning fossil fuels and deforestation. The consequences of this change are already being felt, with rising global temperatures, melting ice caps, and more frequent extreme weather events.

In the United States, the debate over climate change often falls along political lines, with some politicians and interest groups denying the science behind it. However, the overwhelming majority of climate scientists agree that human activities are driving climate change and that urgent action is needed to mitigate its effects. This includes reducing greenhouse gas emissions, transitioning to renewable energy sources, and investing in infrastructure to adapt to a changing climate.

Despite the political divide, there is growing recognition among the American public that climate change is a serious threat that must be addressed. Polls consistently show that a majority of Americans believe that the government should take action to address climate change, whether through regulations on carbon emissions or investments in clean energy technologies. Grassroots movements such as the youth-led Sunrise Movement and the climate advocacy group 350.org have also been instrumental in raising awareness and pushing for policy changes at the local, state, and national levels.

In recent years, there have been some positive developments in the fight against climate change. The Obama administration implemented the Clean Power Plan, which aimed to reduce carbon emissions from power plants, and the Paris Agreement, an international accord that committed countries to reducing their greenhouse gas emissions. However, these efforts have been rolled back under the Trump administration, which has taken a more pro-business approach to environmental regulation.

As we look to the future, it is clear that addressing climate change will require a coordinated effort from governments, businesses, and individuals. By working together to reduce our carbon footprint, invest in clean energy technologies, and adapt to a changing climate, we can help ensure a sustainable future for generations to come. Climate change is a complex issue, but with informed and engaged citizens, we can make a difference.

Chapter 7: The Future of American Democracy

Challenges Facing American Democracy

One of the biggest challenges facing American democracy today is the issue of political polarization. With the rise of social media and cable news networks, people are increasingly retreating into echo chambers where they only hear viewpoints that align with their own. This has led to a decrease in civil discourse and an increase in tribalism, making it difficult for people to come together and find common ground on important issues.

Another challenge facing American democracy is the influence of money in politics. With the Supreme Court's Citizens United decision in 2010, corporations and wealthy individuals are able to pour unlimited amounts of money into political campaigns, drowning out the voices of ordinary citizens. This has led to a system where politicians are more beholden to their donors than to their constituents, undermining the principles of a representative democracy.

Furthermore, there is a growing sense of disillusionment and apathy among the American public when it comes to politics. Many people feel that their voices don't matter and that the political system is rigged against them. This can lead to low voter turnout and a lack of engagement in the democratic process, which is essential for a healthy democracy to function.

Additionally, the issue of gerrymandering poses a significant challenge to American democracy. Politicians in power often redraw electoral districts in a way that benefits their own party, making it difficult for the opposing party to win elections. This leads to a lack of competitive races and can result in elected officials who are not truly representative of the population they serve.

Finally, the spread of misinformation and disinformation online has made it increasingly difficult for people to separate fact from fiction. With the rise of fake news and conspiracy theories, it can be hard for voters to make informed decisions and hold their elected officials accountable. Addressing these challenges will require a concerted effort from all Americans to uphold the principles of democracy and ensure that our political system remains fair and transparent.

The Role of the Average Person in Preserving Democracy

In a democratic society, the role of the average person is crucial in preserving the foundations of democracy. As citizens, we have the power to shape the direction of our country through our participation in the political process. While it may seem overwhelming at times, it is important to remember that each individual has the ability to make a difference.

One of the most fundamental ways that the average person can contribute to preserving democracy is by exercising their right to vote. By casting a ballot in elections at all levels of government, we are able to have a say in who represents us and the policies that are put in place. This simple act is essential in ensuring that our voices are heard and that our government remains accountable to the people.

Additionally, staying informed about current events and political issues is key to being an active participant in democracy. By reading the news, attending town hall meetings, and engaging in discussions with others, we are able to make informed decisions and contribute to the dialogue surrounding important issues. This knowledge empowers us to advocate for policies that align with our values and hold our elected officials accountable.

Furthermore, getting involved in our communities through volunteering, advocacy, or joining local organizations can also have a significant impact on preserving democracy. By working together with others who share our values and goals, we are able to amplify our voices and push for positive change. These grassroots efforts are often where real progress begins, and they demonstrate the power of collective action in shaping our democracy.

In conclusion, the role of the average person in preserving democracy is essential to the health and vitality of our society. By voting, staying informed, and getting involved in our communities, we can ensure that our democratic values are upheld and that our government remains responsive to the needs of its citizens. Each individual has the power to make a difference, and by working together, we can build a more inclusive and participatory democracy for all.

Ways to Stay Informed and Engaged

In today's fast-paced world, staying informed and engaged in American politics is more important than ever. With so much information available at our fingertips, it can be overwhelming to know where to start. In this subchapter, we will explore some simple and effective ways for the average person, teachers, and students to stay informed and engaged in the political process.

One of the easiest ways to stay informed is by following reputable news sources. Whether it's a traditional newspaper, online news outlet, or social media platform, make sure to verify the credibility of the source before trusting the information. By staying up-to-date on current events, you can better understand the issues facing our country and make informed decisions when it comes time to vote.

Another way to stay informed and engaged is by attending local political events and town hall meetings. These events provide an opportunity to hear directly from elected officials and community leaders, ask questions, and voice your concerns. By participating in these events, you can make your voice heard and play an active role in shaping the future of your community.

For teachers looking to engage their students in American politics, incorporating current events into lesson plans can be an effective way to spark interest and encourage critical thinking. By discussing real-world examples and encouraging students to form their opinions, teachers can help students become informed and engaged citizens who are prepared to participate in the democratic process.

Finally, for students looking to stay informed and engaged in American politics, getting involved in student government or political clubs can provide valuable hands-on experience. By participating in debates, organizing events, and advocating for issues they care about, students can develop a deeper understanding of the political process and make a difference in their school and community. By taking these simple steps, the average person, teachers, and students can stay informed and engaged in American politics and play an active role in shaping the future of our country.

Conclusion: Empowering Yourself in American Politics

In conclusion, empowering yourself in American politics is crucial for the health and success of our democratic system. As an average person, teacher, or student, you have the power to make a difference by staying informed, engaging in discussions, and participating in the political process. By understanding how our government works and the role each individual plays in shaping policy and decisions, you can become a more effective and empowered citizen.

One way to empower yourself in American politics is to educate yourself on key political issues and current events. By staying informed through reliable sources of news and information, you can form your own opinions and contribute to meaningful discussions with others. Teachers can also play a critical role in empowering students by incorporating civics education into their curriculum and encouraging critical thinking and active participation in the political process.

Furthermore, getting involved in local and national politics through volunteering, attending town hall meetings, and contacting your elected representatives can have a significant impact on shaping policies that affect you and your community. By voicing your concerns and advocating for change, you can help influence decisions that align with your values and priorities. Remember, democracy is a participatory system, and your voice matters.

It is also important to remember that empowering yourself in American politics is an ongoing process. By continuously educating yourself, engaging with others, and participating in the political process, you can become a more informed and effective citizen. By working together with others who share your values and beliefs, you can make a meaningful impact on the direction of our country and

the future of our democracy.

In conclusion, empowering yourself in American politics is not only

a responsibility but also an opportunity to make a positive difference

in our society. By taking the time to educate yourself, engage with

others, and actively participate in the political process, you can

become a more informed and empowered citizen. Democracy is a

collective effort, and by working together, we can create a more just,

inclusive, and prosperous society for all.